T

THE
DINOSAUR
QUESTION
AND
ANSWER
BOOK

From *OWL* Magazine and the Dinosaur Project

Written by Sylvia Funston

Little, Brown and Company
Boston   Toronto   London

This book was published with the generous support of the Canada Council and the Ontario Arts Council.

The author and publisher extend their thanks to the staff of the Ex Terra Foundation for their assistance, and especially to John Acorn, whose help was invaluable.

The Ex Terra Foundation, a nonprofit organization based in Edmonton, Alberta, Canada, is the sponsor and coordinator of the Dinosaur Project, a joint scientific venture between Canada and China. Three of these countries' most prestigious scientific institutions, the Canadian Museum of Nature, Ottawa; the Royal Tyrrell Museum of Palaeontology, Drumheller, Alberta; and the Institute of Vertebrate Paleontology and Paleoanthropology, Beijing, China, are scientific partners in the Dinosaur Project. Chief paleontologists of the project are Dr. Philip Currie of the RTMP, Dr. Dale Russell of the CMN and Prof. Dong Zhiming of the IVPP. The governments of Canada and Alberta have provided ongoing support and seed monies for both the scientific and public programs of the Dinosaur Project, including *The Dinosaur Question and Answer Book*. The assistance of the above and all those who have helped is most gratefully acknowledged.

First U.S. Edition 1992

In the field of paleontology, new discoveries are constantly being made and theories modified. The information contained in *The Dinosaur Question and Answer Book* is believed by experts to be correct at the time of printing.

First published in Canada in 1992 by Greey de Pencier Books

ISBN 0-316-67736-1
Library of Congress Catalog Card Number 91-59004
Library of Congress Cataloging-in-Publication information is available.

Joy Street Books are published by Little, Brown and Company (Inc.)

10 9 8 7 6 5 4 3 2 1

Art direction and design: Julia Naimska
Design concept: Julie Colantonio

Printed in Hong Kong

Introduction

If you could ask any one question about dinosaurs, what would it be? That's what *OWL* and *Chickadee*—two popular children's magazines—asked their readers across North America. And more than 11,000 questions poured in.

This book answers the questions that came up most frequently. It also answers many remarkable questions that will make you think about dinosaurs in new and exciting ways. In fact, it contains the answers to some puzzlers that have had dinosaur experts scratching their heads in wonder. Do you know the length of *Apatosaurus*'s intestines? Or which dinosaur would make the best pet?

Who provided the information to answer all these questions? The scientists of the Dinosaur Project. To find out more about the Dinosaur Project, read on.

What is the Dinosaur Project?

he Dinosaur Project began in 1984 when some well-known Canadian scientists contacted leading Chinese scientists. Together they decided to mount several dinosaur hunting expeditions, which quickly became the biggest dinosaur hunt in history. After five summers of digging in remote, fossil-rich locations in Asia and North America, more than 40 scientists and technicians had carefully uncovered thousands of bones and found at least 11 completely new kinds of dinosaurs—some of the most exciting finds in the history of paleontology.

▲ Canadian paleontologist Philip Currie pieces together the foot bones of a newly discovered Gobi Desert theropod.

What did the Dinosaur Project hope to discover?

he hunt was on to find new types of dinosaurs as well as fossils of other types of animals and plants that would help create a clear picture of what life was like during the time of the dinosaurs. The team also hoped to uncover clues that would tell them how closely related Chinese and North American dinosaurs might have been. You'll find many of their discoveries throughout this book.

What was the most exciting discovery?

ach scientist who was involved with these expeditions would give you a different answer, so maybe you should decide for yourself. You can choose from 11 new types of dinosaurs. These include the oldest member ever seen of the troodontid family as well as new species of *Psittacosaurus* and Chinese theropods (two-legged meat-eaters). Or perhaps you would choose the 12 young armored dinosaurs found huddled in the Gobi Desert (see pages 10, 30 and 36). And, as you'll soon see, that's not all. . . .

Where did the scientists dig for dinosaurs?

hey decided to look in the Gobi Desert of China, the Canadian Arctic and the badlands of southern Alberta. The Gobi Desert and the Alberta badlands are well-known dinosaur hunting grounds. But the Arctic might surprise you. It was chosen because it might contain clues to an intriguing mystery, which the Dinosaur Project team hoped to solve. You can discover more about this mystery on page 37.

▶ (inset) The Dinosaur Project field camp on Axel Heiberg Island in the Canadian Arctic.

▶ Members of the Dinosaur Project team at work on the fossil-laden rocks of the Junggar Basin in northwestern China.

What was it like working in the Gobi Desert and the Arctic?

t was like going on a camping trip and picking the worst possible place to camp. In the desert, water was scarce, sandstorms came out of nowhere, tents blew away, and the temperature soared each day and plunged at night. Team members had to work hard every day, crawling around on hot, rocky surfaces, hoping they wouldn't get sick from heatstroke. And if that wasn't enough, they also had to give up showers and pizza for months!

In the Canadian Arctic, instead of battling sandstorms, heatstroke and blow-away tents, the team had to contend with snow, total isolation and clouds of biting insects.

Are you a Dino-Buff?

Before you look at any more questions about dinosaurs, find out how much you already know about them. This quiz will reveal your true Dino-Buff rating.

1. What is a dinosaur?

a. A lizard with a crazy walk.
b. A special type of land reptile that lived millions of years ago in the late Triassic, the Jurassic and the Cretaceous periods.
c. A long-legged crocodile.

2. Where did dinosaurs come from?

a. They arrived on a spaceship.
b. They turned overnight from lizards into dinosaurs.
c. They evolved gradually from a group of ancient reptiles called thecodonts.

3. Where did dinosaurs live?

a. In many different environments—ranging from swamps to forests to deserts—on every continent of Earth.
b. In big caves.
c. On the slopes of volcanoes.

4. When did dinosaurs live?

a. They didn't—they're a myth.
b. The first true dinosaur appeared about 215 million years ago. Dinosaurs lived on Earth for the next 150 million years.
c. Sometime between the invention of the wheel and the first video game.

5. Did some dinosaurs live in the sea?

a. Some tried, but the salt hurt their eyes too much.
b. No, dinosaurs never lived in the sea.
c. Yes, but the waves made them seasick.

6. Were the flying pterosaurs a type of dinosaur?

a. Yes, the type that was not afraid of heights.
b. No, they were a type of adventurous flying fish.
c. No, they were a special type of reptile that flew.

7. Are dinosaurs related to crocodiles?

a. No, their closest relatives are bumblebees.
b. No, they're second cousins to jellyfish.
c. Yes, they're distantly related.

**11. If you were a
paleontologist, what
would you study?**

a. Ancient life on Earth. *K S*
b. Ancient life on other planets.
c. Ancient life in other galaxies.

**8. What other kinds of
animals were alive
during dinosaur times?**

a. Besides many other kinds of
animals, there were also living
at that time the ancestors of
every animal on Earth today.
b. With all those dinosaurs
galumphing around, there was
no room for other animals.
c. Only tree-dwelling animals that
were masters of disguise.

**10. Did all the different
kinds of dinosaurs live
at the same time?**

a. Yes, and it got very crowded.
b. No, dinosaur species evolved
and became extinct throughout the entire 150-million-year
period that they were on Earth.
c. Yes, and they had terrible
family squabbles.

**12. What does the word
dinosaur mean?**

a. Noisy, bad-tempered beast.
b. Hungry monster.
c. Terrible lizard. *K S*

**9. What were the two
main groups of
dinosaurs called?**

a. Bird-hipped and lizard-hipped.
b. Bird-lipped and lizard-lipped.
c. Bird-footed and lizard-footed.

Dino-score

Give yourself a point for each
correct answer. (Answers: page 64.)

0–4 Room for improvement.
Better make that room
enough for *Seismosaurus*.
5–8 You're on the right track.
Careful you don't fall into
a huge footprint left by
Mamenchisaurus.
9–12 What a Dino-Buff! You'd
know exactly what to do
if you were being chased
by *Troodon*. Well,
wouldn't you?

Why are names of dinosaurs so complicated?

hy would scientists want to give any self-respecting dinosaur as complex a name as *Micropachycephalosaurus hongtuyanensis*? Because that name describes it perfectly.

Take the first word. *Micro*, *pachy*, *cephalo* and *saurus* are Greek words meaning "small thick-headed reptile." Add to this the second word, which describes the red rock formation where the dinosaur was found. Then the entire name means "the small, thick-headed reptile from the place with red rocks," which is in Laiyung, Shandong, in China. Whew! What could be clearer than that?

How would you say *Micropachycephalosaurus* in Russian, Chinese or French? Exactly the same way. Scientists all over the world use the same Greek or Latin names to describe plants and animals. *Micropachycephalosaurus* was named in 1978 by a leading Chinese dinosaurologist and member of the Dinosaur Project team, Dong Zhiming.

Were there many types of dinosaurs?

magine one species of dinosaur separating into two groups that live in different places. Over a million or so years, the two groups can change so much that they evolve into two different species. If this sort of split happens regularly, after 150 million years you should have billions of species of dinosaurs. Yet, because different species of dinosaurs became extinct over the years, there were probably no more than a few thousand species at most. Of course, no one knows how many new species of dinosaurs are still buried—waiting to be discovered, just like the ones on the opposite page.

Dinosaur Jumble

Whoops! Somebody mixed up the meaning of these dinosaur terms. Can you unscramble them?

tri	foot
dino	big
mega	tyrant
pod	tooth
micro	reptile
tyranno	terrible
donto	small
saur	three

Answers: page 64.
For more about dinosaur words,
check the glossary on pages 60–63.

▲ Dong Zhiming, seen here working on a stegosaur backbone, has named more than 20 dinosaurs since 1973.

All the fossils on this page belong to new species of dinosaurs—some so new they haven't even been named yet.

◀ The squashed original of this model of a cantaloupe-size egg was found in the Alberta badlands. It belonged to a new species of *Hypacrosaurus*.

▶ These three vertebrae belong to a Chinese theropod that was as big as *Albertosaurus*.

▲ Here is a close-up of the foot bones shown on page 4. They belong to a new Chinese theropod related to *Yangchuanosaurus*. (See page 22.)

▶ (top) This cast shows a hatchling *Hypacrosaurus* that would have grown a hollow crest on its head, as do several other kinds of duckbilled dinosaurs.

▶ (bottom) This *Pachyrhinosaurus* skeleton is the size of a large dog. The dinosaur was less than a year old when it died.

How do you know where to look for dinosaurs?

Dinosaurs lived between 215 million and 65 million years ago, so if they are going to turn up anywhere, it will be in rocks of the same age. But not just any old rocks—areas of sedimentary rocks, formed out of layers of mud, sand or gravel, are best. Paleontologists look for these on geology maps. And because digging for dinosaurs is hard work, they look for exposed sedimentary rocks that have been worn away by the weather or running water. With luck, erosion will have done some of the hard work for them, and they might even find fossils sticking out of the ground.

Eighty million years after a sandstorm buried 12 young *Pinacosaurus* in the Gobi Desert, their skeletons were discovered by the Dinosaur Project team.

Why did dinosaurs get buried?

Most animals that die don't become buried. Either they are eaten by predators or scavengers, or their entire carcasses—bones and all—are decomposed by millions of bacteria and other tiny organisms in the air and soil. But the dinosaur skeletons that are being dug up today were buried before they had a chance to decompose. Some got buried under huge landslides, others ended up on river bottoms where they were quickly covered in silt, and others were buried by sandstorms in the desert.

How do you get dinosaur bones out of the rock?

Some of the rocks in the Gobi Desert are so hard that the Dinosaur Project team had to blast them open with dynamite. A *Tyrannosaurus rex* was dug out of a rockface in Crowsnest Pass, Alberta, with jackhammers. There are other, less noisy ways of getting dinosaur bones out of rock. If you're fortunate enough to find small fossils in limestone, you can usually chisel out a chunk of fossil-bearing rock. It can then be soaked in a weak acid bath in the laboratory. The acid eats away the limestone, leaving behind the fossils.

To discover some other tools of the dinosaur-bone-digging trade, solve the puzzle on the next page.

▼ Here is an artist's impression of the 12 young *Pinacosaurus* as the blowing sand overcomes them.

▲ Sometimes you've got to blast through tons of rock to get at well-buried dinosaurs.

What kinds of tools do paleontologists use?

We asked a dinosaur hunter to assemble some of the tools and equipment used during the Dinosaur Project's last expedition into the Gobi Desert. Can you identify the objects in the picture by matching them up with the descriptions of how they're used?

burlap

brush

▲ Dinosaur Project technician Kevin Aulenback uses a scalpel to scrape rock from the skull of a young, sheep-size *Pinacosaurus* in the Gobi Desert.

1. Used to measure fossils and distances between them while they are in the ground.

2. Used to remove large amounts of hard rock above or around the fossil, but *not* right next to the fossil.

3. Used to record each step in the process of taking a fossil out of the ground. It is important for scientists to know how the bones were lying and what kind of rock surrounded them.

4. Used to remove sand and dust from the fossil, once you have removed most of the rock.

5. Used to strengthen the fossil, so it doesn't crumble when you take it out of the ground.

6. Used to examine small fossils, such as teeth and scales.

7. Used like a miniature jackhammer to remove small amounts of hard rock from the fossils.

8. Coated with plaster of paris to make "jackets" to protect large or fragile fossils while they are transported to the laboratory.

9. Used to remove small amounts of rock, to clear off layers of sediments, and as a climbing tool.

10. Used to lift heavy jacketed fossils. Sometimes a helicopter has to lift extra-large jacketed fossils out of rough terrain.

Answers: page 64.

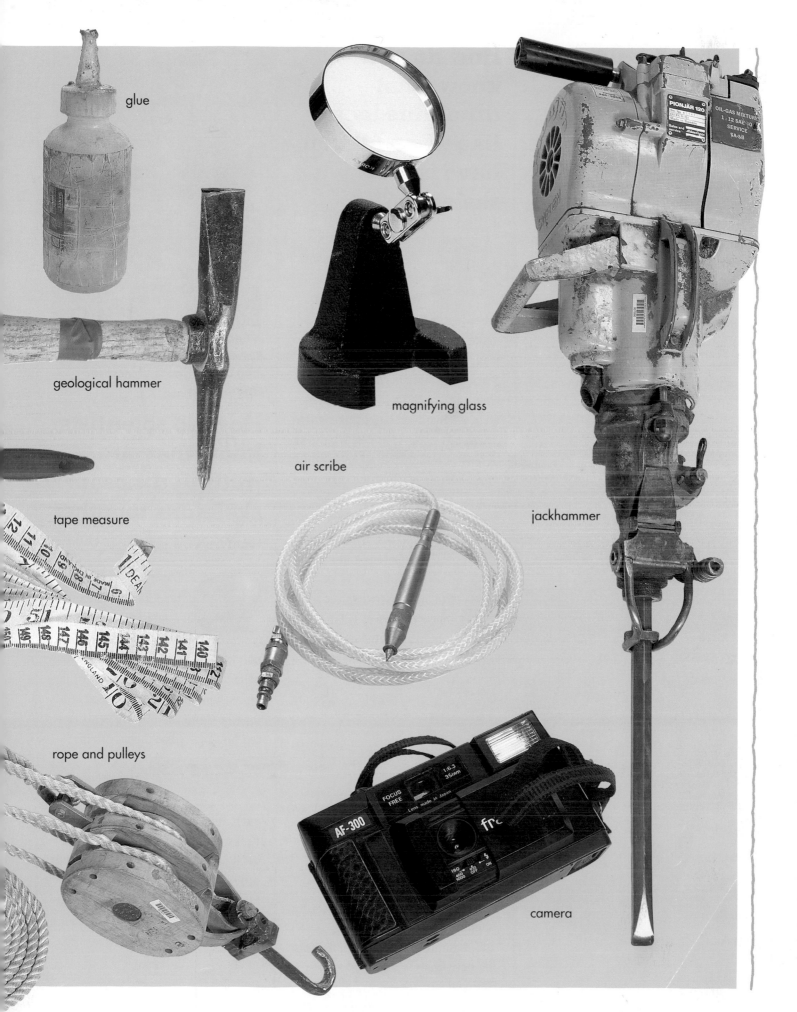

glue

geological hammer

magnifying glass

air scribe

tape measure

jackhammer

rope and pulleys

camera

13

What do dinosaur bones feel like?

If you've ever eaten chicken wings or drumsticks, you know that bones are hard and smooth. They are also light-weight, because they are filled with air holes. But a 65-million-year-old dinosaur bone comes out of the ground a lot heavier than it was when it went in because it has fossilized. In this process, water full of dissolved minerals seeps into the bone, slowly turning it to stone. And stone weighs more than bone.

How do you know what dinosaurs look like when all you have is their skeletons?

Recently, scientists found a skeleton with some fossilized muscle tissue. Finding other fossils like this one could make it easier to know for certain what dinosaurs really looked like. For now, scientists can use clues from the skeletons to figure out what each animal looked like when it was alive. For instance, wherever a muscle attaches to a bone, you'll find a bump on the bone. Also, most animals with four limbs have the same types of bones in similar places. By studying how the skeletons and muscles of modern animals work, paleontologists can get a clear picture of what a living, moving dinosaur must have looked like.

▲ Canadian paleontologist Dale Russell sorts through some *kong long* bones. (That's Chinese for dinosaur.)

How do scientists know they are putting dinosaur skeletons together correctly?

Dinosaur bones fit together in the same way as any other animal skeleton, so it's not difficult to tell where each bone belongs. But sometimes bones from more than one dinosaur get mixed together, and then it's difficult to tell how many backbones or ribs each animal should have. At other times, a skeleton might be missing vital pieces. An *Apatosaurus* stood around for years at the Carnegie Museum of Natural History in Pittsburgh wearing another sauropod's head until its own was discovered.

▲ Philip Currie compares the length of his lower leg with that of the new Chinese theropod whose foot you saw on pages 4 and 9.

"Black Beauty" claw

"Black Beauty" toe bones

The bones of a *Tyrannosaurus rex* from Alberta turned black when magnesium compounds from groundwater seeped into them while they were being fossilized. Scientists dubbed the skeleton "Black Beauty."

◄ When it was time to assemble this life-size replica of *Mamenchisaurus* so that it could be photographed, the Dinosaur Project team realized they didn't have a room big enough for the job. They solved the problem by erecting the four-story-high skeleton outside.

Mamenchisaurus skeleton

Why haven't many baby dinosaur bones been found?

Most dinosaurs have been discovered in areas that were once lush, wet lowlands. Very few baby skeletons have been found in these areas, probably because their fragile bones would rot in the damp before they had a chance to fossilize. Sure enough, recent finds of fossilized dinosaur babies and eggs have all been made in drier upland areas. Finding baby dinosaurs is also easier now that paleontologists know what to look for and can recognize baby dinosaurs instead of assuming that their bones belong to other sorts of small reptiles.

Why did huge dinosaurs lay such small eggs?

Hypacrosaurus was long enough that if you parked a school bus beside one, there wouldn't be much bus sticking out at either end! Yet the female laid eggs that were no bigger than large cantaloupes. Why didn't she lay bigger eggs?

There comes a point where you can't make an egg any bigger because the bigger the egg, the thicker its shell must be. A really thick shell would prevent oxygen from reaching the embryo inside. And hatchlings would need a hammer and chisel to break out! In the case of eggs, then, bigger isn't always better.

Did any dinosaur give birth to babies instead of laying eggs?

ive birth might have been possible for certain dinosaurs, such as wide-hipped *Apatosaurus*. After all, not all reptiles lay eggs. Many, including garter snakes, rattlesnakes and some chameleons, give birth to live young. And scientists have found several fossilized skeletons of an ancient marine reptile called *Ichthyosaurus* that contained unborn young.

Did dinosaurs sit on their eggs to hatch them?

f you weighed more than two fat hippos, would you sit on your eggs? Not likely! But if dinosaurs didn't sit on their eggs, how did they keep them warm? Some duckbilled dinosaurs laid eggs in bowl-shaped mounds. Today, most crocodiles and some birds lay eggs in similar kinds of nests. And they cover them with sand and plants. As the plants rot they give off heat, which incubates the eggs. Did dinosaurs cover their nests? Dinosaur eggs contained so many tiny pores that if they had been exposed to air, they would have dried up inside.

◄ This model of a *Protoceratops* baby hatching shows what a struggle it must have been for most dinosaurs to break out of their tough-shelled eggs.

How large were dinosaur eggs?

f you cracked open a *Hypselosaurus* egg—nonfossilized, of course—you could make scrambled eggs for 36 people. On the other hand, the smallest egg found to date contained a tiny *Mussaurus*. Its eggs were so small, they'd get lost in the bottom of your eggcup. In between there were many sizes—and shapes. Both *Maiasaura* and *Hypacrosaurus* laid eggs that were about two-and-a-half times longer than a large chicken egg, but *Maiasaura's* eggs were lopsided ovals, while *Hypacrosaurus's* were ball-shaped.

A bird colony is a busy, noisy place at hatching time. Imagine what a dinosaur nesting ground must have been like.

A paleontologist made this exact copy of a *Maiasaura* hatchling. The poorly formed joints of the original fossil told experts that this young dinosaur must have been quite helpless when it hatched.

Orodromeus hatchlings were so well developed that they could run around as soon as they broke out of their eggs.

Were baby dinosaurs helpless when they hatched?

ome were as helpless as newly hatched sparrows; others could run around as soon as they were out of the egg, like chickens can. Duckbill hatchlings, for instance, had poorly formed joints and bones, and their nests were full of trampled eggshells—proof that they spent a lot of time in them. Baby hypsilophodonts, however, had strong, fully formed bones and joints. They did not stay in their nests long enough to trample anything. This is why their eggshells are found today in one piece with just a hole in the top where the get-up-and-go hatchlings popped out and went.

Were baby dinosaurs cute?

t's impossible for any infant—whether it's a kitten, your baby sister or a baby rhinoceros—to be anything but cute. A soft, small body, big eyes and poor coordination are all part of being a baby. So the chances are good that if you went time traveling and came across a baby dinosaur, it would be cute enough to make you want to smile.

 A Dinosaur Project technician works patiently to free a nest of *Protoceratops* eggs from rock in the Gobi Desert. This parrot-beaked dinosaur laid 12 or more elongated eggs in a spiral, making sure that each egg stood upright.

If your weight increased between birth and adulthood by the same amount as a duckbilled dinosaur's did, you'd end up weighing as much as four intercity buses!

How big was a baby dinosaur compared with its parents?

ow much did you weigh when you were born? By the time you're fully grown, you will have multiplied your birth weight by 20 times, give or take a few pounds. Newly hatched duck-billed dinosaurs were so tiny compared with their parents that they had to put on a 16,000-fold growth spurt to reach the same weight as their mom or dad.

Did dinosaurs look after their young?

 hese *Hypacrosaurus* hatchlings were the size of small poodles and completely helpless. One or both parents must have looked after them and kept them supplied with berries and tender shoots to eat. And the adults also had to stay alert to danger and hope that it didn't arrive in the shape of a hungry *Albertosaurus*.

Which dinosaur would make the best pet?

 f your backyard was the same size as Central Park in New York, a small herd of *Apatosaurus* would be ideal. You'd need a lake and a year-round supply of fresh vegetation for them. But because they were used to a warm climate, you'd have to house them each winter in a building about half the length of a football field—which you'd have to keep clean! If all this sounds like too much work, perhaps one of the

small carnivores, or meat-eaters, such as *Troodon* would be right for you. Given *Troodon*'s speed, intelligence and appetite for small, warm, furry objects, though, it would be wise not to let it play with the neighbors' gerbils!

Like *Troodon*, the two

most popular pets today

are both small carnivores.

How much would it hurt if a plant-eating dinosaur bit you?

 eing bitten by *Parasaurolophus* (right) would hurt as much as if you stuck your fingers in an automatic food grinder. These dinosaurs didn't just have a single set of dentures. They had interlocking rows of teeth that formed a continuous grinding surface. First they'd bite; then they'd grind. Ouch!

Is it true that one small dinosaur fought with karate kicks?

ot one, but several small meat-eating dinosaurs had a huge sickle-shaped claw on each back foot, which would have been deadly when used with a karate-like kick. *Velociraptor* from Mongolia was one; *Troodon* and *Deinonychus* from North America were two others. Some scientists think that *Deinonychus* hunted in packs. Part of the pack would grab hold of the victim's tail while the others delivered slashing kicks to the soft underbelly of their prey. You'll find a dynamic kick-boxing duo on page 23.

Parasaurolophus skull

One type of plant-eating hadrosaur had 2,000 teeth!

Did any baby dinosaurs have baby teeth?

aby hadrosaurs (duckbilled plant-eaters) have been found, still in their eggs, with tiny, perfectly formed baby teeth. Luckily, they didn't lose them all at once. Like all dinosaurs, hadrosaurs lost a tooth here and a tooth there and grew replacements for them all through their lives.

What kind of temperament did dinosaurs have?

las, it's impossible to tell from a bunch of old bones whether they held up a ferocious beast or a gentle creature. For all we know, *Mamenchisaurus* might have had a mean streak as long as its neck. Then again, it could have been as docile as a dove.

Which were the most ferocious dinosaurs?

What a tough question! We've organized a freestyle wrestling match that pits the fiercest theropods of all time against one another. You can decide the winners.

On this side, representing the Jurassic period (193 to 136 million years ago), are:

▶ **Mighty** *Megalosaurus* from England, France and Morocco. "Mighty M" leads with its teeth and has some head-locking strong-arm tactics to be reckoned with. Will any opponent in the ring today be able to knock this tenacious broad-beamed fighter off its feet?

Yikes! *Yangchuanosaurus* from China. ▶ Rumor has it that "Yahoo Yang" breaks trees in half to stay in shape. It might not be the flashiest fighter in the ring, but its bulldog determination, stupendous strength and lethal feet help this tyrant fight to win.

Awesome *Allosaurus* from ▶ North America. Watch for "Awesome's" flexible neck work in the clinches. And those powerful arms with big claws are built for grappling and ripping. Ouch!

And here, representing the Cretaceous period (136 to 65 million years ago), are:

Treacherous *Troodon* ▶
from Alberta and Montana. This sharp-eyed fighter is one of the smartest around and specializes in lightning-fast rip-attacks. When the going gets slippery, "Treacherous T's" ribbed teeth are perfect for grabbing hold and hanging on.

Villainous *Velociraptor* ▶
from China. It might be small, but pound for pound "Villainous Velo" is one of the most powerful fighters around. Watch for its triple combination attack with teeth, hands and sickle claws, as well as its specialty: the double drop-kick.

Terrible *Tyrannosaurus rex*
from Alberta, Montana, Saskatchewan, Texas and Wyoming. "Born-to-Bite" *T-rex* earned its nickname the snappy way. And look out for some punishing blows to its opponent's head from those sharp-edged hornlets over its eyes. ◀

Will the agility and speed of the little guys in *T-rex*'s corner make up for the sheer brute power of Mighty *Megalosaurus*'s gang? Only you can decide.

Which was the smallest dinosaur?

hat was smaller than a speeding lizard, had two pincer-like fingers on each arm and had a name that means "pretty jaw"? *Compsognathus*, the tiniest meat-eating dinosaur of them all. Even when it was fully grown, *Compsognathus* weighed only as much as a newborn human baby. If it were around today, it would be able to stare a rooster in the eye without bending down.

Are blue whales bigger than dinosaurs?

es. Blue whales are the biggest animals that have ever lived on Earth. Animals can grow much bigger in the sea than they can on land because everything weighs less under water, just as it does in space. How big is a blue whale? At least 22 times heavier than *Tyrannosaurus rex* and slightly longer than one side of a baseball diamond. To find out what would happen to a land-stomping dinosaur if it got that big, see page 46.

How big was *Apatosaurus*'s intestine?

hen you're fully grown, your small intestine will be about 3½ times as long as you are tall. If *Apatosaurus* were the same, its small intestine would be 99 feet long, but scientists think it may actually have been 10 times that length. *Apatosaurus* needed a long intestine, and maybe even one with many large pouches, to store its hard-to-digest plant food for extra-long periods of time so the bacteria inside could help break it down.

How long was the longest dinosaur neck?

Of all the dinosaurs, *Mamenchisaurus* had the longest neck, with an average one measuring about 33 feet long. Recently, however, the Dinosaur Project team found more than a dozen *Mamenchisaurus* neck bones that belonged to a huge neck that would have reached 46 feet on the tape measure. The dinosaur that owned it was probably just over twice as long as its neck. If this stretched-out sauropod ever tried to board a school bus, its head would hit the back window before its front feet even got past the driver's seat.

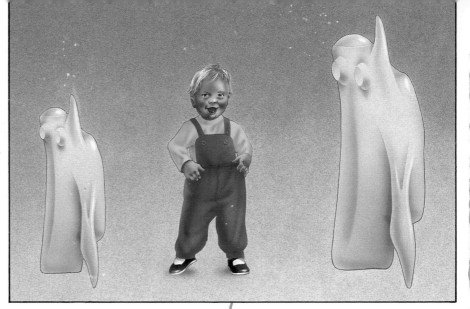

Seismosaurus, discovered in 1986, might have a longer neck, but the skeleton is still partially buried. Sound pictures taken through rock show that it is almost twice as long as *Mamenchisaurus*! How much of its length is neck, no one knows.

▲ The *Mamenchisaurus* neck bone on the left is about 2 feet long. The new one found by the Dinosaur Project is almost 3 feet long. We've compared them with a year-old baby to show you how big they are.

▼ *Mamenchisaurus* is often shown with its head out in front, but it probably held it high like a giraffe.

Is it true that some dinosaurs had two brains?

on't laugh. There's some truth to this rumor. What they had, however, wasn't so much a second brain as a large swelling of the spinal cord above their hips. The spinal cord is the thick bundle of nerves that connects the brain to every part of the body through a network of nerves. The swelling, or ganglion, acts like an automatic control center for parts of the body far away from the brain. It was especially important in large animals such as *Stegosaurus* that had to control huge back legs and use their tails as weapons.

All animals with backbones have this ganglion, and insects have many of them.

A bird's-eye X-ray view (above) of this *Stegosaurus* and a wood-boring beetle shows that the dinosaur has one ganglion to help control its movements whereas the beetle has many of them.

brain

spinal column

ganglion

brain
spinal column

ganglia

wood-boring beetle

Stegosaurus

Stegosaurus

How smart were dinosaurs?

ould you describe a crocodile or an alligator as dim-witted? If so, you'd have to call most dinosaurs dim-witted, too, because they probably had as much brainpower as today's reptiles. Some of the small theropods—*Troodon, Oviraptor, Avimimus* and *Ornithomimus*—had larger-than-average dinosaur brains. It's thought that they were as smart as *Archaeopteryx*, the world's first bird. Now, if *Archaeopteryx* had the IQ of a chicken, that wouldn't have been much to boast about. But if it was as clever as a raven, then that would be something indeed.

If I stepped on a big dinosaur's tail, how quickly would it react?

ow's your math? Pain messages travel along nerves at speeds of 20 to 80 inches per second. The longest dinosaur of them all, *Seismosaurus*, is thought to have been about 145 feet long. If you stepped on *Seismosaurus*'s tail, it could take as long as 1½ minutes before the message finally reached its brain. If *Seismosaurus* stepped on *your* toe, you'd say "Ouch!" a lot faster than that.

The small, carnivorous *Troodon* is considered by many paleontologists to be one of the smartest dinosaurs of them all.

How big was *Tyrannosaurus rex?*

yrannosaurus rex was so tall that if you stood on a grown-up's shoulders, you would not even reach the level of its hips. *T-rex* was so long that it could bite the diving board in most backyard pools while hanging on to the wall at the shallow end with its tail. And *T-rex* was so heavy that if it climbed on one side of a seesaw, you'd have to balance the other side with 86 full-grown men!

Were tyrannosaurs the original "airheads"? Some scientists think that the air canals in these dinosaurs' skulls were used to pump air from their lungs to cool their brains. Others think they improved hearing and reduced the weight of the immense tyrannosaur head.

How wide could *Tyrannosaurus rex* open its mouth?

sk a *Tyrannosaurus rex* to say "Aah," and its mouth would open as wide as a bathtub. But get out of the way before its huge jaws snap shut! Those lethal weapons could take a chunk bigger than two kitchen sinks out of an unlucky *Triceratops*.

Tyrannosaurus rex skull

▲ This skull belonged to "Black Beauty," a *T-rex* found in Alberta. (See page 15.)

Did any other dinosaur have bigger teeth than *Tyrannosaurus rex* did?

o other dinosaur has been unearthed that had teeth as impressive as those flashed by a grinning *T-rex*. Its biggest teeth were as long as dinner knives

and had a row of tiny bumps and grooves on their front and back edges. These serrated edges acted like thousands of pairs of open scissors slicing into prey. Its front teeth acted like cookie cutters—perfect for scooping out big chunks of meat.

▼ *T-rex* was constantly growing sharp new teeth to take the place of the old ones it shed.

Tyrannosaurus rex tooth

◀ The illustration below will help you pick out the shapes of *Proto-ceratops* and *Velociraptor* in this photograph. The battling pair were discovered in Mongolia by Polish paleontologists.

Protoceratops

Velociraptor

Did dinosaurs eat one another?

hen the Dinosaur Project team found 12 young *Pinacosaurus* in the Gobi Desert (see pages 10 and 36), it was clear that two theropods, *Velociraptor* and *Saurornithoides*, had been feeding on them. They had even left behind some of their teeth. *Velociraptor* had turned up before in the Gobi Desert, locked in combat with a horned dinosaur, *Protoceratops*. *Velociraptor* had obviously attacked *Protoceratops*, which in defense had clamped its jaws around *Velociraptor*'s arm. Whatever happened, *Velociraptor* was not about to let go of a potential dinner.

Dinosaurs lived and died without ever seeing grass. Fossils show that it didn't appear until long after they became extinct.

Did dinosaurs eat mice?

lthough the ancestor of mice lived at the same time as the dinosaurs did, real mice and other rodents didn't appear until 10 million years or so after the dinosaurs died out. So dinosaurs couldn't have eaten mice. But there were strange rodent-like mammals around at that time called multituberculates, which small theropods such as *Troodon* probably hunted.

▶ Leaf fossils offer clues about ancient climates. Large tooth-edged leaves tell of cool, wet weather; small spiny ones survived dry conditions. Long, slender leaves grew in windy spots, and smooth-edged ones with tips that allow water to drip grew in warm, damp places. You may recognize these plants since most still grow today.

Monkey
Puzzle

Cycad

Ginkgo

Did dinosaurs make big droppings?

This coil-shaped dropping, or coprolite, is a mere 3 inches long and may have come from a small, meat-eating dinosaur. Droppings from giant plant-munchers have been difficult to identify because they lack definite shape.

A geologist from California, however, has recently studied some irregular blocks of black rock containing fossilized plant material. She claims they might well be *Maiasaura* droppings. If they are, they will tell scientists exactly what plants this dinosaur considered a tasty meal.

English Laurel

Magnolia

Did dinosaurs sit down to eat vegetation or low branches?

Does a rhinoceros sit down to eat grass, or a giraffe squat to nibble on low branches? No, and for good reason. A rhino's head is close to the ground because that is where all of its food grows. A giraffe's head is at the end of a long neck, close to leaves high in trees. Substitute *Triceratops* for the rhino and *Diplodocus* for the giraffe, and you can see how these two dinosaurs fed. And they'd have as little reason to sit down as do the rhino and the giraffe.

Fern

Horsetail

Yew

Pine

How can you tell whether each dinosaur ate plants or meat?

Very occasionally, a dinosaur hunter will find a dinosaur whose stomach contents have been fossilized. Usually, however, they use other detective skills to determine dinosaur diets.

For instance, big mouths full of sharp teeth suggest that their owners attacked and ate other animals. After all, if you went to the zoo at feeding time, you wouldn't expect to see lions and tigers contentedly munching on bales of hay.

On the other hand, mouths full of grinding teeth point to animals that had to chew tough vegetation. When was the last time you saw a cow with a wicked set of canines?

Even the shape and size of the dinosaur's body provide useful clues. A big head and jaws and a powerful, stocky neck belong on a meat-eater. And a long neck and small head belong to a plant-eater that browses among the treetops.

Try your sleuthing skills on these teeth and figure out whether they belong to a meat-eater (carnivore) or plant-eater (herbivore). But be careful. One set of teeth belongs to a dinosaur that scientists think might have eaten both meat *and* plants (an omnivore).

Answers: page 64.

▲ **Massospondylus** had a mouth full of small, triangular, coarse-edged teeth that look as if they could either grip, slice or grind. These teeth belong to: **a.** A carnivore.   **b.** An herbivore.   **c.** An omnivore.

▲ This relative of **Yangchuanosaurus** has sharp, serrated teeth that curve backward to give it a better grip on its meal. These teeth belong to: **a.** A carnivore. **b.** An herbivore. **c.** An omnivore.

All of **Diplodocus**'s pencil-like teeth are at the front of its long, weak jaws. No good for chewing, they were probably used for raking. These teeth belong to:
a. A carnivore. **b.** An herbivore. **c.** An omnivore.

Edmontosaurus's battery of sharp, diamond-shaped teeth act like a giant food grater to grind up tough food. These teeth belong to:
a. A carnivore. **b.** An herbivore. **c.** An omnivore.

Psittacosaurus didn't have many teeth, but its long, sharp beak could slice easily through tough, fibrous materials. These teeth belong to:
a. A carnivore. **b.** An herbivore. **c.** An omnivore.

33

How can you tell meat-eaters' and plant-eaters' footprints apart?

irst check to see if the animal walked on two or four feet. Most meat-eating dinosaurs walked on two feet (*Baryonyx* was a possible exception) and left sharply pointed bird-like prints with three toes. Any dinosaur that walked around on four feet usually ate plants. However, some plant-eating duckbills and hypsilophodonts and some members of the pachycephalosaur and heterodontosaur families walked around on two legs when it suited them.

The dinosaurs below look confused. And no wonder! The footprints they have left behind don't belong to them. Can you match up each dinosaur with its correct footprints?

Answers: page 64.

Elephants walk around on tiptoe. A shock-absorbing wedge of spongy tissue beneath each heel lifts them off the ground. Sauropods had the same type of spongy wedge beneath their heels.

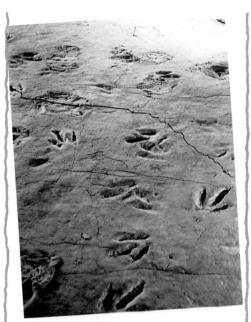

▲ A cast of a duckbilled dinosaur footprint found in the Peace River Canyon, British Columbia.

◀ Tracks found in Connecticut's Dinosaur State Park resemble those made by *Dilophosaurus*.

Could dinosaurs swim?

ootprints are the only evidence we have that some dinosaurs may have swum. But if you swam across a river or a lake, would you leave footprints on the bottom? Not unless your feet occasionally touched the riverbed or lakebed. Scientists think that those sorts of tracks are what they have found. Under the right conditions, these footprints could become fossils. Impressions of claw tips have been found that look as if they were made by a swimming theropod called *Dilophosaurus*. And tracks of only the front feet of a large sauropod suggest that either it was very good at handstands or it was swimming with its rear end buoyed up by the water. A single print from one of its back feet shows where it kicked out to change direction, and it seems to support the idea that sauropods, at least, were better swimmers than acrobats.

A single *Apatosaurus* footprint found in Colorado measures 2 feet across and over 3 feet long. It can hold enough water to bathe a young child.

Can you tell how fast dinosaurs moved?

f scientists know the length of a dinosaur's back leg from foot to hip and the distance between its footprints, they can make a rough estimate of how fast it was walking when it made those footprints. Next time you go to the beach or cross muddy ground, check to see what happens to your footprints when you walk, then run. The faster you move, the longer your stride becomes. Your stride is the distance from any one of your footprints to the next print made by the same foot. Try making tracks with friends whose legs are longer or shorter than yours and compare the results. And don't forget to note the depth of your prints as you speed up or slow down.

Match the Movers

Paleontologists figured out how fast some well-known dinosaurs moved compared with some modern animals, but their results got jumbled up. Can you match up each animal with its correct speed?

Edmontosaurus	18 mph
African elephant	40 mph
Hypsilophodont	26 mph
Tyrannosaurus rex	12 mph
Racehorse	18 mph
Coelurus	26 mph
Ostrich	9½ mph

Answers: page 64.

Did young dinosaurs stay with their parents?

aleontologists have found an enormous herd of duckbilled *Maiasaura* that were killed by a heavy fall of volcanic ash. The herd was made up of four distinct sizes of dinosaurs. Some scientists think that the two smallest sizes were babies and youngsters, and the two largest, teens and adults. If this is so, *Maiasaura* grew up with the herd.

The group of young *Pinacosaurus* that you met on page 10, however, appeared to have been traveling separately from their herd. No adult skeletons were found nearby. Of course, this could mean the youngsters were with a herd but were dawdling. It could also mean that any adults with them were able to dig themselves out after the sandstorm.

▲ In China the Dinosaur Project team found the tiniest dinosaur fossil ever: a 6½-inch-long *Pinacosaurus* that probably died before it hatched.

A "dinosaur highway" containing more than a million footprints of plant-eating dinosaurs was recently discovered running north-south along the eastern edge of the Rocky Mountains.

The barren landscape of Bylot Island in the Canadian Arctic makes it difficult to believe that it was once so full of plant life that dinosaurs found it a good place to live.

Did dinosaurs migrate?

n expedition to Bylot Island in the Arctic brought the Dinosaur Project team closer to solving the mystery of whether some dinosaurs migrated each year.

The team already knew that *Pachyrhinosaurus* remains had been discovered south of the Arctic, in Alaska and in northern and southern Alberta. If dinosaur fossils also could be found in the High Arctic, they would provide stronger evidence that dinosaurs migrated in search of food. Why? Even though the Arctic climate was milder then than it is now, Arctic winters were just as long and dark. Plants would become dormant for many months. How then could plant-eating dinosaurs survive unless they migrated south?

In the summer of 1989, the remains of plant-eating hadrosaurs discovered by the Dinosaur Project team on Bylot Island finally proved that dinosaurs lived in the High Arctic. The discovery also makes it highly probable that they migrated south each autumn, as herds of caribou do today, to where the sun shone all winter and plants continued to grow.

A herd of *Maiasaura* desperately tries to outrun a rolling cloud of volcanic ash.

How did dinosaurs get all over the world?

hen dinosaurs first evolved, they could have strolled from the Arctic to Antarctica if they chose without crossing a single sea. In those days, the Earth's seven continents were all joined together as one super landmass, which we now call Pangaea. But Pangaea began to split up about 150 million years ago, and the continents started their slow drift apart. Obviously, dinosaurs were moved around with the drifting continents. But there's evidence that they also traveled from continent to continent on their own two or four feet. They followed the land connections that appeared when sea levels fell, particularly between North America, Asia and Europe.

▶ **70 million years ago, North America was divided by a great sea. A strip of land connected western Canada and China.**

If the continents drifted apart at the rate of only 4 inches a year, after 150 million years they'd have traveled 9,000 miles.

Are the dinosaurs of North America related to Chinese dinosaurs?

ou're a small dinosaur chomping on tasty plants in Wyoming 70 million years ago. You look up to see a *Tyrannosaurus rex* striding purposefully in your direction. How you wish you were far away in China. But don't be too hasty with those wishes! In China, you'd be just as likely to look up into the welcoming grin of a creature that could stand in as a movie double for *T-rex*. It's the deadly *Tarbosaurus bataar*.

Are these two look-alikes related? They lived at a time when North America and Asia were joined

Tyrannosaurus rex

Mamenchisaurus (left) was wandering around China 150 million years ago while *Diplodocus* (below) was sticking its neck into things in North America. Yet as much as these two sauropods look alike, they are unrelated. At the time they evolved, North America and Asia were separated by ocean.

together. Almost all the dinosaur families found in North America at that time are also found in China. They're not exactly alike, but close enough to suggest strong family ties. The Dinosaur Project team sees this as further evidence of dinosaur movement between the two continents.

Tarbosaurus bataar

Did any dinosaurs have trunks?

lephant skulls have holes in the top for their noses. But their nostrils are at the end of a long trunk that sticks out of the front of their faces, not the top of their heads. Sauropods such as *Diplodocus* and *Brachiosaurus* had nose holes on top of their skulls too. Does this mean that they had trunks that grew from the front of their faces? We might never know. Noses, cheeks, lips and ears don't last long enough to fossilize. So go ahead and imagine *Brachiosaurus* with an enormous trunk or your favorite hadrosaur with floppy ears if you wish.

Little *Triceratops* hatched from their eggs looking quite round and cuddly—well, maybe their parents thought so. Fossils show that these dinosaurs didn't grow their impressive horns until they were young adults—between two and four years old.

Why were some dinosaur heads so small?

ut yourself in the place of *Brachiosaurus* for a minute. You're one of the biggest animals that ever lived, yet your head looks as if it were designed for an animal no bigger than a horse. You've also got an extremely long neck that needs plenty of muscle power to hold it up. Imagine how much more difficult it would be to hold up your long neck and head all day if that head were monstrously big like the rest of you. A small head made life a lot easier for *Brachiosaurus*.

Why did some duckbilled dinosaurs have crests on their heads?

h, dear. You're a *Lambeosaurus* with a problem. You've got to choose a mate, but all the distinctive crests of the different types of duckbills that live close by are hidden. Can you pick out your *Lambeosaurus* mate from this group of dinosaurs?

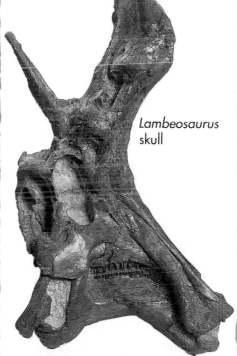

Lambeosaurus skull

You've just seen how crests helped dinosaurs recognize others of their own species. But did you know that crests were also hollow? When the dinosaur breathed, each breath of air went through the crest. Perhaps different-shaped crests produced different sounds. Their large size might even have increased the duckbills' sense of smell.

Without those telltale crests, it's not easy. Now try again.

Were dinosaurs warm-blooded or cold-blooded?

 warm-blooded animal, such as a tiger, generates its own body heat from the large amounts of food it eats. It can be active whenever it wants, for long periods of time.

A cold-blooded animal, such as a snake, can't make its own heat, so it must absorb heat from the sun or its surroundings. It doesn't require as much food as a warm-blooded animal, but it can be active only for as long as it stays warm.

Many scientists now agree that small meat-eating dinosaurs were probably warm-blooded. But most big dinosaurs could have been cold-blooded animals whose sheer bulk helped them stay warm all the time. Here's how it works.

The leatherback turtle is a big, cold-blooded reptile that spends most of its time in warm tropical waters, where it has no problem staying warm. But the leatherback

▲ Some scientists think that small predatory dinosaurs may have grown feathers for insulation. Here's what *Velociraptor* might have looked like.

manages to stay warm even when it visits the cold northern waters of the Atlantic. This turtle is so big that heat stored deep inside its body takes a long time to reach the surface and radiate out into the water. And an insulating layer of blubber just beneath its skin helps prevent further heat loss. If a one-ton leatherback turtle can stay warm in cold surroundings, surely a dinosaur 10 times its weight with much greater heat storage capacity could easily do the same.

▶ (opposite) You can clearly see the outline of feathers in the rock around this fossil of *Archaeopteryx*, the oldest known bird.

Did some dinosaurs have fur or feathers?

 ome paleontologists claim that small, warm-blooded dinosaurs might have used feathers as insulation to keep their temperatures stable in hot or cold weather. Unfortunately, no dinosaur fossil has been found that shows feathers. But that doesn't mean that none exists. The oldest known bird, *Archaeopteryx*, had feathers, but only four of the six *Archaeopteryx* fossils found show impressions of feathers.

As for fur, none has been found on a dinosaur fossil. But a crow-size pterosaur called *Sordes pilosus* left an impression in limestone of what *looks like* dense fur on its body. Its wings and tail were naked, like those of a bat. Because none of the other pterosaur fossils showed fur, however, many scientists are still undecided about the possibility that there were furry pterosaurs.

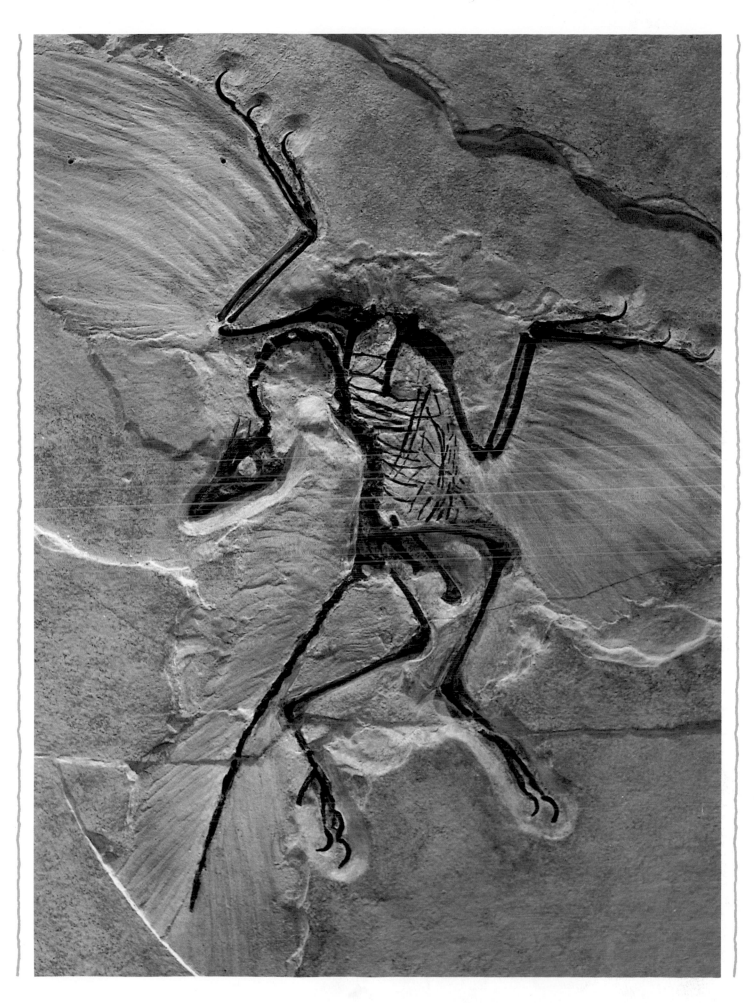

Is it true that some dinosaurs had armor?

 f a *Tyrannosaurus rex* mom gave her offspring one piece of advice, it surely must have been, "Think twice before biting an *Ankylosaurus*." The large, bony plates, called scutes, embedded in the skin of this armored tank of a creature were hard enough to break the strongest teeth. So how could *T-rex* attack *Ankylosaurus*? By flipping the tank onto its back. *Ankylosaurus* didn't carry any belly armor.

What color were dinosaurs?

 here are plenty of theories, but no absolute proof, about the color of dinosaurs. Color pigments usually disappear when skin becomes fossilized. A recent find in New Mexico, however, has got scientists hoping that one day they'll dig up a dinosaur with well-preserved skin color. What raised their hopes? A fossilized turtle shell as strikingly red and black today as it must have been 70 million years ago.

Meanwhile, most scientists agree that dinosaurs were probably colored or patterned much as animals are today. Modern animals use color and patterns to attract a mate,

▼ This fossilized, tooth-breaking scute would have been one of many embedded in an armored dinosaur's skin.

Albertosaurus

frighten off would-be attackers, or camouflage themselves. Here's how four types of familiar animals camouflage themselves. These illustrations show what dinosaurs would have looked like if they had done the same.

▲ Spots and Stripes

Leopards and tigers have patterned coats that make them difficult to see against the contrasting light and shade of their forest surroundings. Dinosaurs that lived in similar settings might have had similar patterns and colors.

Dark and Light ▶

Have you noticed how many animals—ranging from killer whales to antelopes and hawks—have a dark back and a pale belly? Land animals with this kind of shading are difficult to see against bright open spaces. The same would apply to small dinosaurs living in similar conditions.

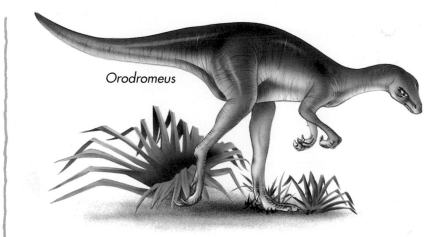

Orodromeus

Parasaurolophus

Brachiosaurus

▲ Little Spots and Stripes

Cougars give birth to spotted babies, and wild boar babies are born with stripes. When these babies remain still on the forest floor, their spots and stripes make them almost invisible. Think how much safer a spotted or striped baby dinosaur would have been if it too lived in a forest.

◀ Too Big to Care

Many big African animals—elephants, rhinos, hippos and crocodiles—are gray all over. They don't need camouflage patterns or color. They rely on their horns, teeth and bulk for protection. Sauropods probably relied on their size and were likely as drab and gray as elephants and rhinos.

How big could a dinosaur get?

If you could magically grow bigger, until you had twice as much skin (what scientists call your surface area), you would find that you weighed far more than twice as much as you used to. If you continued to grow, your weight would increase faster than the strength of the body parts that hold you together. If you, or a dinosaur for that matter, grew too big, your weight would eventually crush your leg bones. As strange as it seems, the bigger you get, the weaker you get. This is probably why dinosaurs never got any bigger than "Ultrasaurus." And it's why elephants, the biggest animals on land today, have got extra-strong leg bones and chunky feet!

"Ultrasaurus" is the biggest dinosaur excavated so far. If it stood on tiptoe, it could peek through the sixth-floor windows in an apartment building. From its nose to the tip of its tail it was as long as three school buses, and it weighed more than 20 elephants.

◀ James Jensen standing beside the colossal front leg of "Ultrasaurus," a huge dinosaur that he discovered in Colorado in 1979.

How do we know dinosaurs didn't live beyond 65 million years ago?

In Alberta's badlands and in other places around the world, you can see layers of rock that are between 65 million and 90 million years old. These layers are full of dinosaur fossils. In the newer rocks immediately above the 65-million-year-old layer, you will find only the skeletons of reptiles and many mammals, but no dinosaur skeletons.

In a few places around the world, single dinosaur bones *have* been found in rocks less than 65 million years old. And at some sites, *Triceratops* teeth have also been dug out of newer rock. But many scientists think that these dinosaur fossils didn't really belong in the newer rocks. It's likely that they got washed out of older levels and were then reburied among newer material.

▲ 65 million years ago, Alberta's Horseshoe Canyon was a sandy delta surrounded by swamp. The sandy areas show up as thick light layers, the swamp as dark bands of coal.

If dinosaurs were so big and strong, why did they become extinct?

It doesn't matter whether you're as small as a water snail or as big and powerful as a polar bear. It doesn't even matter whether you're intelligent or not, fast or slow, warm-blooded or cold-blooded.

Survival of a species has to do with how well all its members can adapt to changes in their environment so that they can go on producing offspring. Dinosaurs obviously weren't flexible enough to adapt to the mysterious changes that swept the Earth 65 million years ago.

Triceratops

47

Which dinosaurs were the first to become extinct?

Dinosaurs began to die out soon after they first appeared more than 200 million years ago. They didn't all wait until 65 million years ago to become suddenly extinct.

The dinosaurs at the top of the page are some of the earliest to evolve and, therefore, among the first to become extinct. As the dinosaurs in each group died out, new ones evolved to take their place. Each step down the page contains more recent dinosaurs. Did *Apatosaurus* ever meet *Tyrannosaurus rex*?

Apatosaurus couldn't have met *Tyrannosaurus rex* because it became extinct 70 million years before *T-rex* came along. In fact, you live closer in time to *T-rex* than *Apatosaurus* ever did!

Dinosaurs that became extinct 200 million years ago

Staurikosaurus

Dinosaurs that became extinct 175 million years ago

Scelidosaurus

Dinosaurs that became extinct 135 million years ago

Mamenchisaurus

Dinosaurs that became extinct 90 million years ago

Brachiosaurus

Dinosaurs that became extinct 65 million years ago

Nemegtosaurus

Massospondylus   Procompsognathus   Herrarasaurus   Coelophysis

Dilophosaurus   Vulcanodon   Segisaurus   Lesothosaurus

Allosaurus   Stegosaurus   Yangchuanosaurus   Apatosaurus

Psittacosaurus   Iguanodon   Wuerhosaurus   "Sinornithoides"

Thescelosaurus   Tyrannosaurus rex   Leptoceratops   Triceratops

Did something from space destroy the dinosaurs?

oday, more scientists than ever are ready to think so. Why? A few years ago, a thin layer of a mineral called iridium was discovered all over the world. Iridium is normally found in much greater concentrations in meteorites and heads of comets than on Earth. This iridium layer was deposited on Earth in the Cretaceous period, 65 million years ago—exactly when the dinosaurs died out. Furthermore, it's full of shocked quartz, which is only produced in colossal explosions.

If, as many scientists think, a comet 6 miles across collided with Earth, it would strike with a force 10,000 times that of all the world's nuclear weapons. The impact would send up such an enormous cloud of dust that it would plunge the whole Earth into darkness. Temperatures would fall, and burned nitrogen in the air would fall to Earth as strong acid rain. It's a wonder anything could survive these conditions, yet one-third of all of the animal species came through the Cretaceous extinction unharmed.

▶ A comet approaches Earth.

▶ (opposite) Ten seconds after impact. Vaporized rock and water rise 60 miles into the atmosphere.

Did volcanoes cause the death of the dinosaurs?

ccording to one interesting theory, volcanoes may have caused the dinosaurs' extinction. If enough volcanoes were spewing lava and ash into the air at the same time, they would have the same effect as the impact of a giant meteor. All of the resulting dust, chemicals, gas and ash would cause significant changes in the Earth's climate.

In some parts of the world, scientists have found areas where lava rock from volcanic eruptions is about half a mile thick. It would take a lot of eruptions to make that much lava rock, and experts think it took place over a period of about 50 million years. But when did all the volcanic eruptions that resulted in this lava rock begin? The first lava began to flow about 65 million years ago—right at the end of the dinosaur age.

How could one disaster kill *all* the dinosaurs?

ot all scientists think there is enough fossil evidence to say for sure that the last dinosaurs disappeared all at once. Some believe that the remaining dinosaurs slowly died out, one species at a time, over thousands or even millions of years.

▲ Arizona's Meteor Crater is a mere 49,500 years old and less than 1 mile across.

If a meteorite collided with Earth and killed the dinosaurs, wouldn't it leave a big crater?

 meteorite or comet capable of doing that much damage would have left a crater 90 miles across. How could we miss something this big? It might have been buried under floods of lava. Or it could be on the sea floor. Several large crater-like areas have been found on the seabed. There's one north of the island of Madagascar and another at the tip of Mexico's Yucatán Peninsula.

Is it possible to clone a dinosaur?

To clone an animal you use the living contents of one of its cells—its DNA—to produce an exact replica of the original animal. When an animal dies and becomes fossilized, all its DNA usually gets fossilized, too, and then it can't be used for cloning. Some scientists think there is an extremely remote chance, however, that a dinosaur might be found in such a good state of preservation that its DNA could be reconstructed to produce a clone.

It would take many decades and more money than has been spent on the U.S. space program to clone a dinosaur. But if you found the right fossil—a dinosaur that got "pickled" in the Alberta tar sands, for instance— it could be done.

Is the legend of a dinosaur in Africa based on a true creature?

Mokele-mbembe is described as a hippo-size, sauropod-type creature that lives in the river systems of northern Congo and southern Chad and feeds on malombo fruit, also known as jungle chocolate. However, there is no proof that this shy, sweet-toothed vegetarian is a real animal, let alone a dinosaur. Paleontologists think Mokele-mbembe stands as much chance of being a dinosaur as it does of being an extraterrestrial.

What would have happened to the dinosaurs if they hadn't died out?

During the last few million years of the dinosaurs' existence, there evolved a small, swift theropod called *Troodon*. It came from an old family of large-brained dinosaurs. *Troodon* ran around on two legs and had three digits on its hands, one of which it could use like a thumb to grasp things. Its eyes were huge. They were also forward-facing, giving *Troodon* good depth perception for hunting.

▲ **Crocodiles haven't changed much since the time of the dinosaurs. If *Troodon* had changed as little, it would look today just as it did 65 million years ago.**

It's possible that this creature wouldn't have evolved much at all. But the model, opposite, shows what Dinosaur Project scientist Dr. Dale Russell thinks *Troodon* might have evolved into if dinosaurs hadn't become extinct.

Which animals have changed the least since dinosaur times?

Welcome to a hot, humid Jurassic swamp 160 million years ago. The animals here, with the exception of the pterosaur, have descendants living today. Some have changed little since Jurassic times, but one might surprise you. Can you match up each animal with its description?

Answers: page 64.

Animal Descriptions

1. Salamanders haven't changed much, and even this ancient one had bright colors.

2. *Archaeopteryx* was a tiny theropod with wings and feathers.

3. Each of *Rhamphorhynchus*'s wings was supported by an enormously long finger.

4. Beetles, like this predatory ground beetle, were very common all through the age of reptiles.

5. This swamp-dwelling crocodile could grow as long as 20 feet.

6. This turtle couldn't pull its head into its shell.

7. This 3-inch-long katydid looked a lot like its living relatives, and even more like a green leaf.

8. This dragonfly had a wingspan of about 8 inches and hunted smaller insects.

9. This ancestor of the snake had short legs.

10. This cat-size mammal, called *Triconodon*, probably laid eggs like a reptile but nursed its young like other mammals.

11. This frog lived mostly on land and was a powerful jumper.

12. This tuatara—the only survivor of an ancient group of reptiles called sphenodontids—ate insects and worms.

Is it true that birds are really dinosaurs?

ext time you stock up your bird feeder, pat yourself on the back for helping to keep a long line of singing dinosaurs alive and flapping. According to the way scientists now classify animals, all the descendants of a particular ancestor are grouped under the same name. Since birds and dinosaurs descended from one particular dinosaur ancestor, they all fall into the same group—dinosaurs. Who that ancestor was remains a mystery, except that it was a small, meat-eating theropod that ran on two legs.

Dinosaurs fit into two major groups. One group had hip bones shaped like those of modern birds; the other had hip bones shaped like those of lizards. You would expect that birds evolved from bird-hipped dinosaurs. But believe it or not, they evolved from lizard-hipped dinosaurs.

Did all dinosaurs turn into birds?

nly one type of dinosaur evolved into birds, and it was a small, meat-eating theropod. All theropods had bird-like bodies. You can easily see this in small theropods such as *Ornithomimus*, *Velociraptor* or *Troodon*. You have to look a little harder to see the bird-like body in *Tyrannosaurus*, but it's true. *Tyrannosaurus* was as bird-like as little *Troodon*. Think of that the next time you sit down to a turkey dinner.

What was *Archaeopteryx*— bird or dinosaur?

ome scientists think that *Protoavis* was the first real bird. Most, however, still believe that *Archaeopteryx*, even though it evolved from a dinosaur ancestor, was the first real bird. But birds can be classed as dinosaurs because they're descended from them. So *Archaeopteryx*, like all other birds, can be called both a bird and a dinosaur.

► Here is one artist's impression of how dinosaurs evolved into birds.

Why did mammals only get big after the dinosaurs became extinct?

 hings balance out well in nature. There is only room for a certain number of big predators and plant-eaters. Unfortunately for mammals, dinosaurs occupied all these positions for 150 million years. As soon as the dinosaurs became extinct, however, mammals were able to take advantage of the territories and food that the dinosaurs no longer needed. The many new species of mammals that arose gradually grew bigger and stronger.

In this scene, you'll find five dinosaurs and five mammals. Can you figure out which mammals took the place of which dinosaurs?

Answers: page 64.

Many mammals are now smaller than their ancestors were thousands of years ago. But not humans. An average, well-fed 12-year-old is as tall today as his or her great-great-grandparents were when they were fully grown.

Hypacrosaurus

Deinonychus

Brachiosaurus

Orodromeus

Tyrannosaurus rex

Where were people during the dinosaur age?

I t's difficult to imagine the world without people, yet it got by until very recently without us. To give you an idea of just how new people are, imagine you're reading a book about the history of life on Earth. This heavy book has 1,000 pages and covers a span of 3½ billion years. The human race—*Homo sapiens*—gets its first mention in the last couple of lines on the very last page, long after you finish reading about the life of the dinosaurs.

People, or *Homo sapiens*, hadn't evolved when dinosaurs were around, but your distant ancestors, the first primates, appeared late in the dinosaur age. Today the dinosaurs are gone, but the primates have remained. Remarkably, one species of primate developed enough brainpower to be able to look back over millions of years and prove that a successful race of super-reptiles once roamed the Earth. The likes of the dinosaurs had never been seen before and will never be seen again. But of all the millions of species that live on Earth today, only yours knows of the dinosaurs' existence—and what an existence it was.

Glossary

Dinosaurs have some of the most awkward names ever invented. But successfully wrapping your tongue around a difficult dinosaur name is half the fun of getting to know them. Besides, you can really impress people by how fast you can rattle off *Micropachycephalosaurus* (remember it from page 8?).

On these pages, you'll find all the Latin and Greek words that make up the names of the dinosaurs and some of the other animals in this book. First you'll see the word, then its origin or the language it comes from, followed by its meaning.

If you want to know what *Protoceratops* means, look down the list until you come to a word beginning with the letters *pro*. You'll find the meaning of *proto*. Next, look for *cerat* and add its meaning onto the first. All that's missing now is the *ops*. Put the three parts together and you get a dinosaur name that means: "first-horned-face" (*proto-cerat-ops*).

All the names here either describe what dinosaurs look like or do, or the place where they were discovered, or occasionally the person who discovered them.

Names of dinosaurs and other creatures

Name	Origin	Meaning	Name	Origin	Meaning
A			**D**		
alberto	place name	Alberta, Canada	*deino, dino*	Greek	terrible (awesome)
allo	Greek	different	*di*	Greek	two
anchi	Greek	near	*diplo*	Greek	twofold
ankylo	Greek	crooked	*docus*	Greek	beam
anuro	Greek	without a tail	*don, dont,*		
apato	Greek	lying, deceitful	*donto*	Greek	tooth
archaeo, archo	Greek	very old	*dromeus*	Greek	runner
avi, avis	Latin	bird			
			E		
B			*edmonto*	place name	Edmonton, Canada
bary	Greek	heavy	*elasmo*	Greek	metal plate
bataar	Mongolian	hero	*ensis*	Latin	place, country, locality
brachio	Greek	arm			
			G		
C			*gnathus*	Greek	jaw
carno	Greek	a type of horn from ancient Gaul			
			H		
centro	Greek	point, midpoint	*hadro*	Greek	large, strong
cephalo	Greek	head	*herrera*	place name	Herrera, Argentina
cerat, ceros	Greek	horn	*hetero*	Greek	other, different
cetio	Greek	monstrous	*hongtuyan*	Mandarin	red rocks
coelo	Greek	hollow	*hypacro*	Greek	below the top
compso	Greek	elegant, pretty	*hypselo, hypsi*	Greek	high
cono	Greek	cone			
copro	Greek	dung, excrement	**I**		
corytho	Greek	helmet	*ichthyo*	Greek	fish
			iguano	Caribbean	iguana lizard

Name	Origin	Meaning
L		
lambe, lambeo	person's name	Lawrence Lambe
lepto	Greek	delicate
lesotho	place name	Lesotho, Africa
lestes	Greek	robber, pirate
lites	Greek	stone
lopho	Greek	crest, ridge
M		
maia	Greek	good mother
mamenchi	place name	Mamenchi, China
masso	Latin	bulk, body
mega, megalo	Greek	great, big
micro	Greek	small
mimus	Greek	imitate
morpho	Greek	shape
multi	Latin	many
mus	Latin	mouse
N		
nemegt	place name	rock layer in Asia
nychus	Greek	claw
O		
oides	Greek	like
onto	Greek	being, thing
onyx, onychus	Greek	claw
ops	Greek	face
ornith, ornitho	Greek	bird
oro	Greek	mountain
ovi	Latin	egg
P		
pachy	Greek	thick
physis	Greek	condition, nature
pilosus	Greek	hair
pinaco	Greek	board, plank
plesio	Greek	near, recent
pod	Greek	foot
pro	Greek	before
proto	Greek	first
psittaco	Greek	parrot
ptero, pteryx	Greek	wing
R		
raptor	Latin	grabbing
rex	Latin	king
rhampho	Greek	curved beak
rhino	Greek	nose
rhynchus	Greek	snout

Name	Origin	Meaning
S		
saur, saura,		
sauro, saurus	Greek	reptile
scelido	Greek	limb
segi	place name	Segi Canyon, Arizona
segno	Latin	slow
seismo	Greek	earthquake
sino	Latin	China
sordes	Latin	dirt, filth
spino	Latin	thorn
spondylus	Greek	vertebra (backbone)
stauriko	Greek	cross
stego	Greek	roof
T		
tarbo	Greek	frightful
theco	Greek	sheath
thero	Greek	summer
thescelo	Greek	wonderful
tri	Greek	three
troo	Greek	wounding
tointao	place name	Tsintao (Qingdao), China
tyranno	Greek	tyrant
U		
ultra	Latin	beyond
urus	Greek	tail
V		
veloci	Latin	swift, speedy
vulcano	Latin	volcano
W		
wuerho	place name	Wuerho, China
Y		
yangchuan,		
yangchuano	place name	Yangchüan, China

Dinosaur Terms

archosaurs — The "ruling reptile" group that consisted of dinosaurs, pterosaurs, crocodilians, birds and their thecodont ancestors.

Cretaceous — The period between 65 million and 144 million years ago, from the Latin word *creta*, meaning chalky. Shallow, warm seas were common during this time, and chalky layers of rock accumulated on their floors.

hadrosaurs — Large, duckbilled plant-eaters that walked on two or four feet.

hypsilophodonts — Medium-size plant-eaters that walked on two feet. They looked like small hadrosaurs, but they weren't duckbilled.

Jurassic — The period between 144 million and 213 million years ago, named for the rocks laid down in the Jura Mountains of France and Switzerland. A time when the super-continent of Pangaea was splitting into two major land-masses.

Ornithischia — One of the two great groups of dinosaurs (*see also* Saurischia), which included plant-eating dinosaurs with horny beaks and leaf-shaped crowns on their teeth. Also known as bird-hipped dinosaurs.

paleontologist — A scientist who specializes in the study of ancient life on Earth.

plesiosaurs — Marine reptiles (not dinosaurs) with paddle-like feet and sharp teeth for eating fish. Some had long necks; others had short necks.

pterosaurs — Flying reptiles (not dinosaurs) with skin wings supported by one very long finger. The smallest ones were sparrow-size; the largest ones were the size of a small airplane.

Saurischia — The second of the two great groups of dinosaurs (*see also* Ornithischia), which included two-legged meat-eating theropods and mainly four-legged plant-eating sauropods. Also known as lizard-hipped dinosaurs.

sauropods — Very large, four-legged plant-eaters with long necks and small heads. Their backbones were often hollowed out to reduce their weight, and their long tails balanced their necks.

thecodonts — Most were four-legged reptiles (not dinosaurs) that were the ancestors and cousins of dinosaurs, pterosaurs and crocodilians.

theropods — Two-legged meat-eating dinosaurs with bird-like bodies. Most had sharp teeth and clawed fingers.

Triassic — The period between 213 million and 248 million years ago, during which three successive layers of rocks were laid down in Germany. During this time, Pangaea was showing its first signs of splitting up.

Index

Answers

Are you a Dino-Buff? (pages 6-7)

1. b. Dinosaurs belonged to a group of "ruling reptiles" called Archosauria.
2. c. One of the earliest known dinosaurs, *Herrerasaurus*, lived in South America.
3. a.
4. b.
5. b. Ocean creatures such as *Elasmosaurus* and other plesiosaurs may have looked like dinosaurs, but they were a different kind of reptile.
6. c.
7. c. Dinosaurs, crocodilians, pterosaurs, birds and their thecodont ancestors formed the "ruling reptile" group.
8. a.
9. a. Meat-eaters (theropods) and long-necked plant-eaters (sauropods) were lizard-hipped dinosaurs. All other plant-eaters were bird-hipped.
10. b.
11. a.
12. c. The name *dinosaur* was invented in 1842 by British scientist Richard Owen. Of course, we now know that they were reptiles, but not lizards.

Dinosaur Jumble (page 8)

Tri: three	Micro: small
Dino: terrible	Tyranno: tyrant
Mega: big	Donto: tooth
Pod: foot	Saur: reptile

Check out the glossary on pages 60-63 for more unusual names.

Paleontologists' Tools (pages 12-13)

1. tape measure	6. magnifying glass
2. jackhammer	7. air scribe
3. camera	8. burlap
4. brush	9. geological hammer
5. glue	10. rope and pulleys

Plant-eaters or Meat-eaters? (pages 32-33)

Massospondylus: c.	*Edmontosaurus*: b.
Yangchuanosaurus: a.	*Psittacosaurus*: b.
Diplodocus: b.	

Footprint Mix-up (page 34)

A: 2, B: 3, C: 4, D: 1

Match the Movers (page 35)

Edmontosaurus: 12 mph	Racehorse: 40 mph
African elephant: 18 mph	*Coelurus*: 26 mph
Hypsilophodont: 9 ½ mph	Ostrich: 26 mph
Tyrannosaurus rex: 18 mph	

Animals from Dinosaur Times (pages 54-55)

All the animals except *Rhamphorhynchus* (C) survived to the present day. Did you identify the crocodile (B), tuatara (F), ground beetle (G), turtle (H), frog (I), salamander (J), katydid (K) and dragonfly (L) as animals that have hardly changed at all in 160 million years? And *Archaeopteryx* (A), apart from its teeth and the claws on its wings, is recognizable as a bird. The squirrel-size mammal, *Triconodon* (D), may have been an ancient ancestor of today's Monotremata—duckbilled platypuses and prickly echidnas. And the lizard (E) might surprise you: it's an ancestor of the snake.

Present-Day Mammals (pages 58-59)

Large predators such as polar bears took the place of big theropods such as *Tyrannosaurus rex*. Smaller predators such as wolves took the place of small theropods such as *Deinonychus*. Big plant-eaters such as elephants took the place of *Brachiosaurus* and other sauropods. Antelopes took the place of *Orodromeus* and other hypsilophodonts, and cows took the place of *Hypacrosaurus* and other hadrosaurs.

Credits

Photography Credits

The following copyrighted photographs were used with permission of the Ex Terra Foundation:
pp. 3, 4, 5, 12, 18 Brian Noble; 5 (inset) R. L. Christie; 8, 11, 14 (upper), 37 Mike Todor; 14 (lower) Alan Bibby/Great North Communications; 36 John Acorn.

The following copyrighted photographs were used with permission of the individual or institution indicated in each case:
p. 30 Wojciech Skarzynski, courtesy of the Institute of Paleobiology, Polish Academy of Sciences, Warsaw; 35 courtesy of Dinosaur State Park, Rocky Hill, Connecticut; 17 Donald Baird (reconstruction by J. R. Horner); 43 Smithsonian Institution, photo No. 856814; 46 © by Mark A. Philbrick, Brigham Young University; 47 Royal Tyrrell Museum/Alberta Culture and Multiculturalism; 51 courtesy of Meteor Crater, Northern Arizona.

All other photographs by Kate Kunz.

Our thanks to the Royal Tyrrell Museum of Palaeontology for permission to photograph the following items from their collection:
title page, skull of relative of *Yangchuanosaurus*; p. 9, model of *Hypacrosaurus* egg; 12-13, paleontology tools; 14-15, cast of *Mamenchisaurus* skeleton; 15, "Black Beauty" bones; 21, *Parasaurolophus* skull; 29, "Black Beauty" skull, *Tyrannosaurus rex* tooth; 31, dinosaur coprolite; 32-33, skulls of *Diplodocus*, *Edmontosaurus*, *Massospondylus*, *Psittacosaurus* and relative of *Yangchuanosaurus*; 35, cast of duckbilled dinosaur footprint; 41, *Lambeosaurus* skull; 44, ankylosaurid scute.

Our thanks to the Institute of Vertebrate Paleontology and Paleoanthropology, China, for permission to photograph the following items from their collection:
p. 9, dinosaur hind foot, dinosaur vertebrae; 36, small fossilized *Pinacosaurus*.

Our thanks to the Ex Terra Foundation for permission to photograph the following items from their collection:
p. 9, *Pachyrhinosaurus* skeleton, cast of *Hypacrosaurus*.

Illustration Credits

pp. 2-3 "*Brachiosaurus*" by Steve Pilcher; 6-7 Dan Hobbs; 10-11 Steve Pilcher; 16 "*Protoceratops*" model © by Sylvia Czerkas; 17 "*Orodromeus* Nesting Site (Egg Mountain)" © by Douglas Henderson; 19 "*Hypacrosaurus* Feeding Young" © by John Gurche; 20-21 Dan Hobbs; 22-23 Graeme Walker; 24-25 "*Mamenchisaurus* Crossing the Flats" © 1986 by Mark Hallett; 25 Graeme Walker; 26 Graeme Walker; 26-27 Graeme Walker; 27 Dan Hobbs; 28 Steve Pilcher; 30 "A Fight to the Death" © 1984 by Mark Hallett with permission of the Natural Wildlife Federation; 31 Graeme Walker; 34 Dan Hobbs; 36-37 © by Doug Henderson, collection of the Museum of the Rockies; 38-39 Graeme Walker; 40 Dan Hobbs; 41 Dan Hobbs; 42 Steve Pilcher; 44-45 Graeme Walker; 47 "*Triceratops*" model © by S. & S. Czerkas; 48-49 Graeme Walker; 50-51 "Extinction of Dinosaurs" by Eleanor M. Kish, reproduced with permission of the Canadian Museum of Nature, Ottawa; 52 "*Troodon*" by Ron Séguin in collaboration with Dr. Dale Russell, reproduced with permission of the Canadian Museum of Nature, Ottawa; 53 "Dinosauroid" by Ron Séguin in collaboration with Dr. Dale Russell, reproduced with permission of the Canadian Museum of Nature, Ottawa; 54-55 Steve Pilcher; 56-57 "Dinosaur into Bird" © 1985 by Mark Hallett; 58-59 Graeme Walker.